4th Grade Math Workbook

Fractions & Geometry Practice

BABY PROFESSOR

EDUCATION KIDS

Speedy Publishing LLC
40 E. Main St. #1156
Newark, DE 19711
www.speedypublishing.com

FRACTIONS

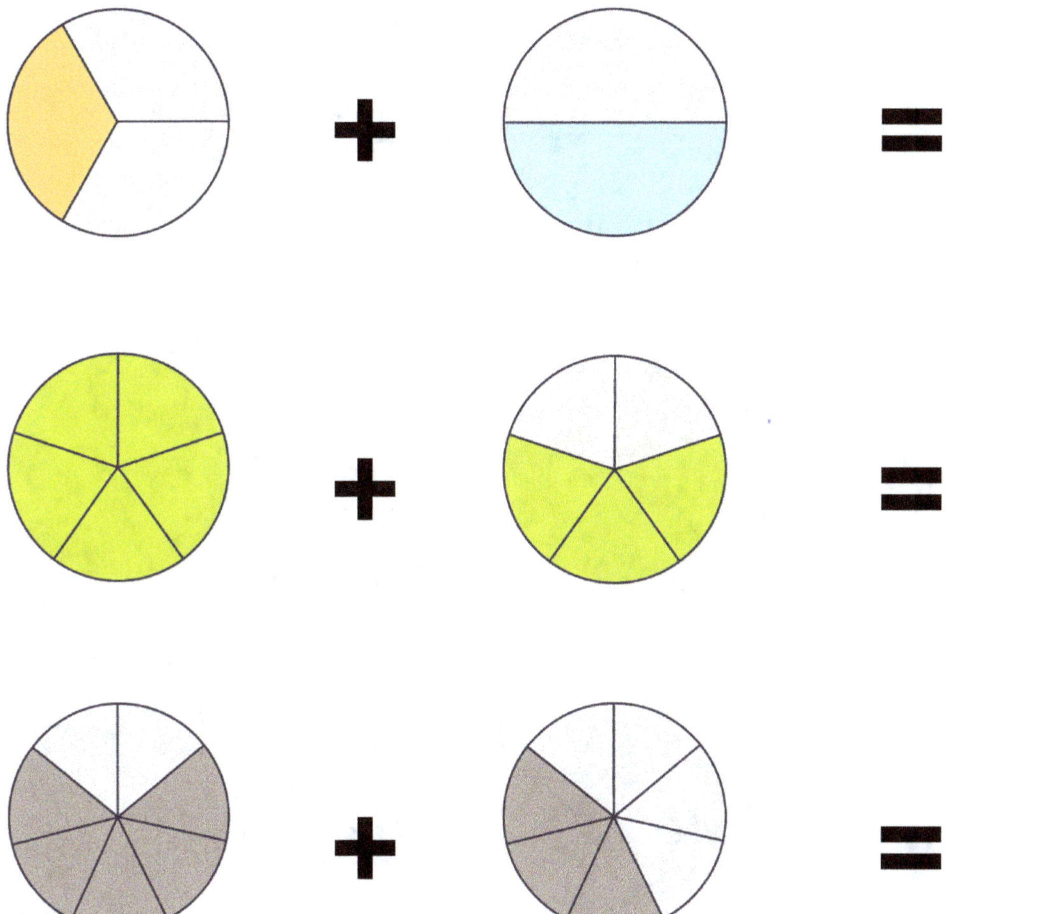

FRACTIONS

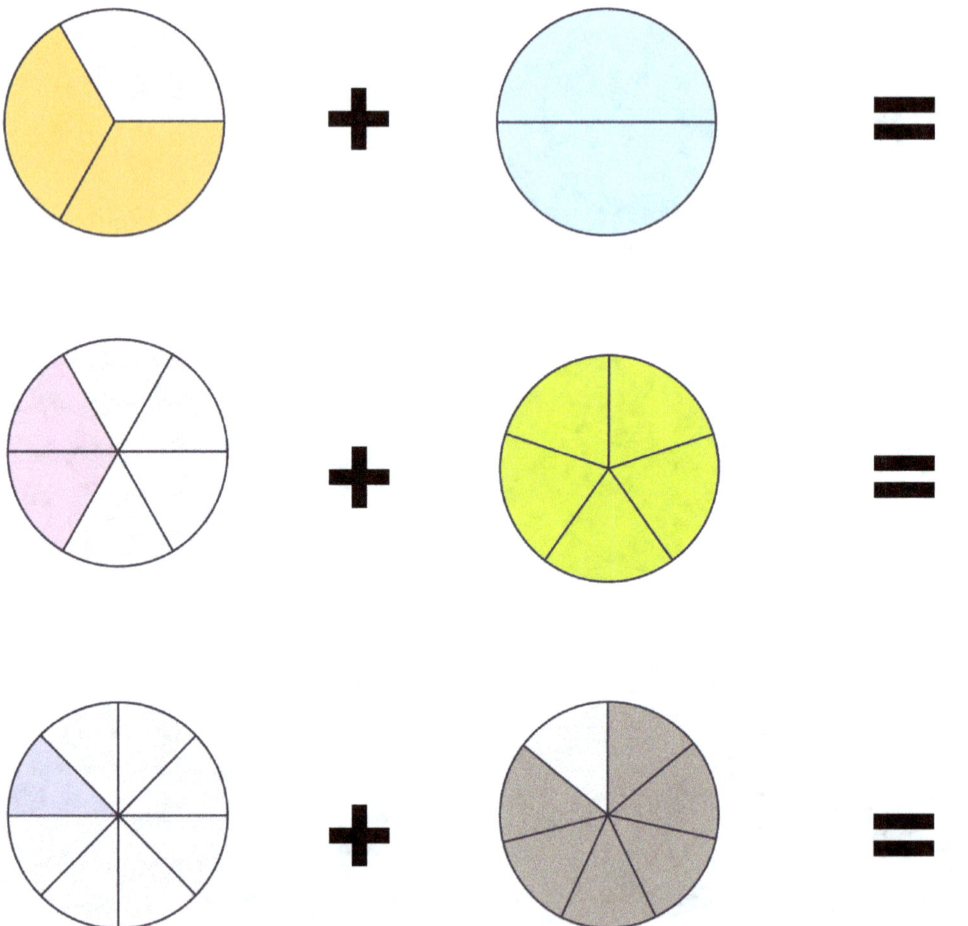

FRACTIONS

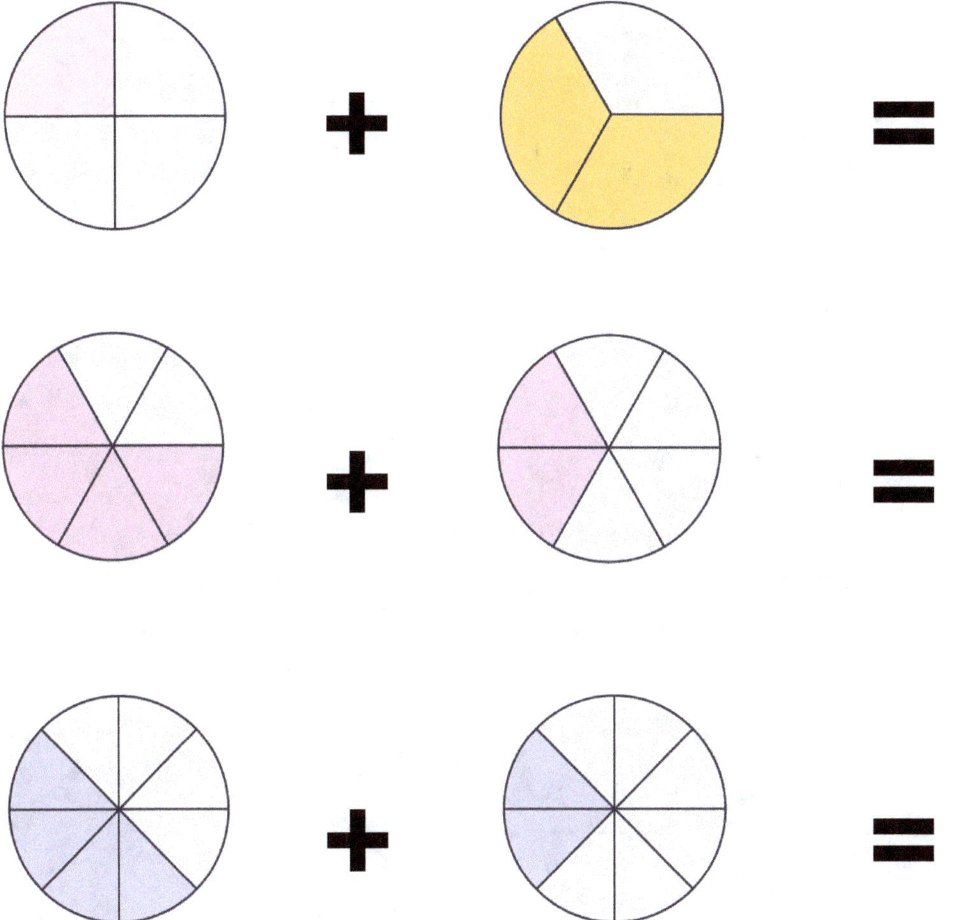

FRACTIONS

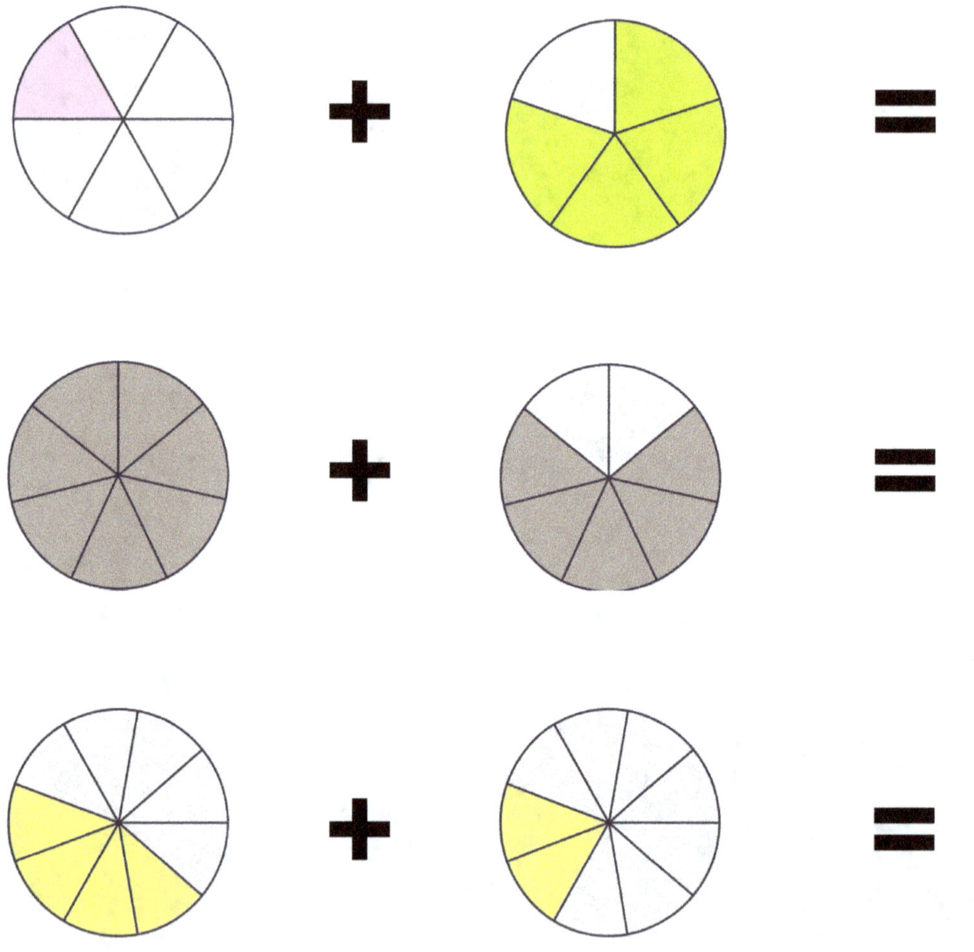

FRACTIONS

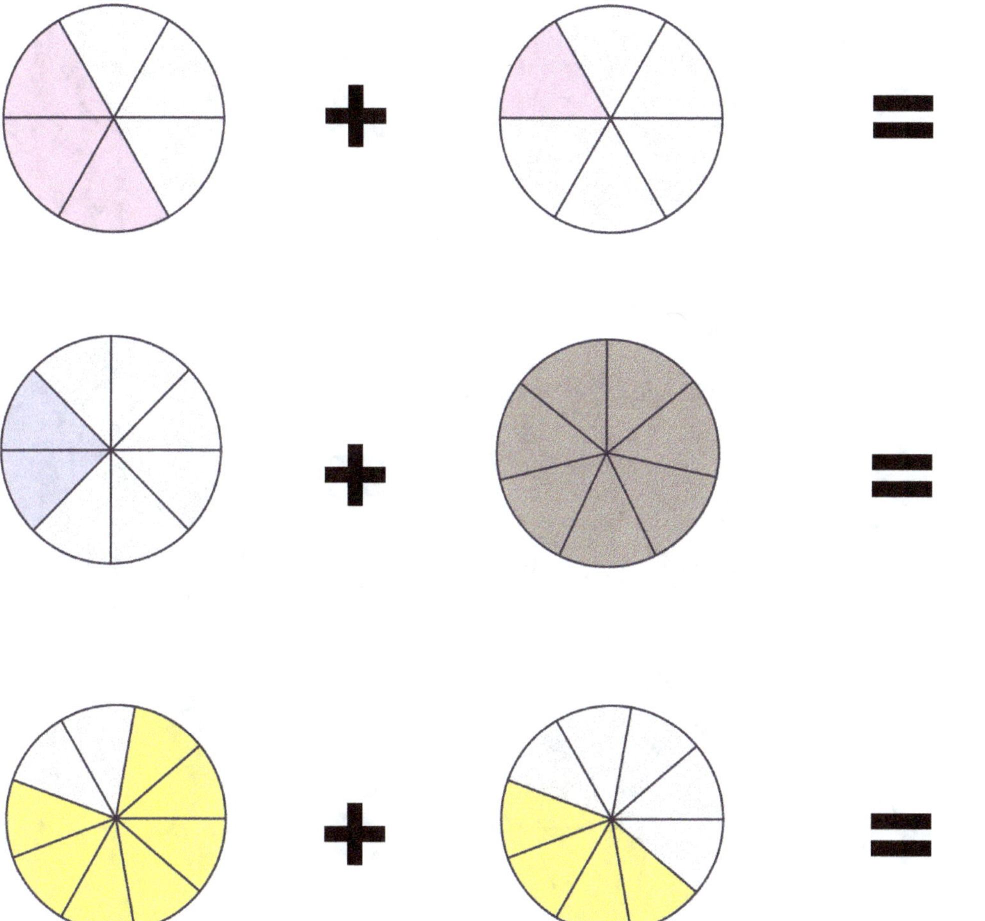

FRACTIONS

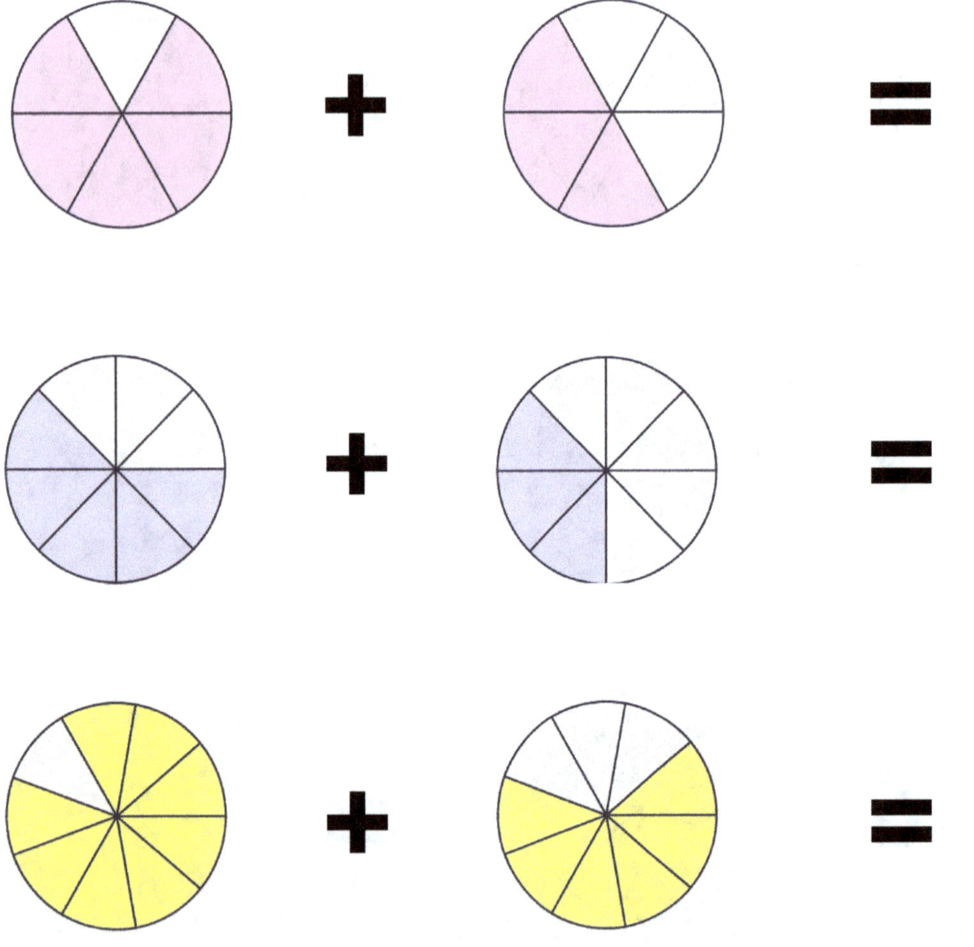

FRACTIONS

2/3   +   1/5   =

1/3   +   2/3   =

4/5   +   2/7   =

FRACTIONS

$$1/4 \quad + \quad 2/5 \quad =$$

$$3/5 \quad + \quad 1/3 \quad =$$

$$1/5 \quad + \quad 1/6 \quad =$$

FRACTIONS

$$1/3 \quad + \quad 2/3 \quad =$$

$$3/4 \quad + \quad 4/5 \quad =$$

$$2/5 \quad + \quad 1/5 \quad =$$

FRACTIONS

4/7 + 4/6 =

1/8 + 2/3 =

3/9 + 2/5 =

FRACTIONS

3/4 + 4/9 =

4/7 + 6/7 =

8/9 + 3/4 =

FRACTIONS

3/4   +   3/4   =

1/4   +   3/4   =

4/6   +   6/7   =

GEOMETRY

Measure the angle and name what type of angle.

____

____

____

____

GEOMETRY

Measure the angle and name what type of angle.

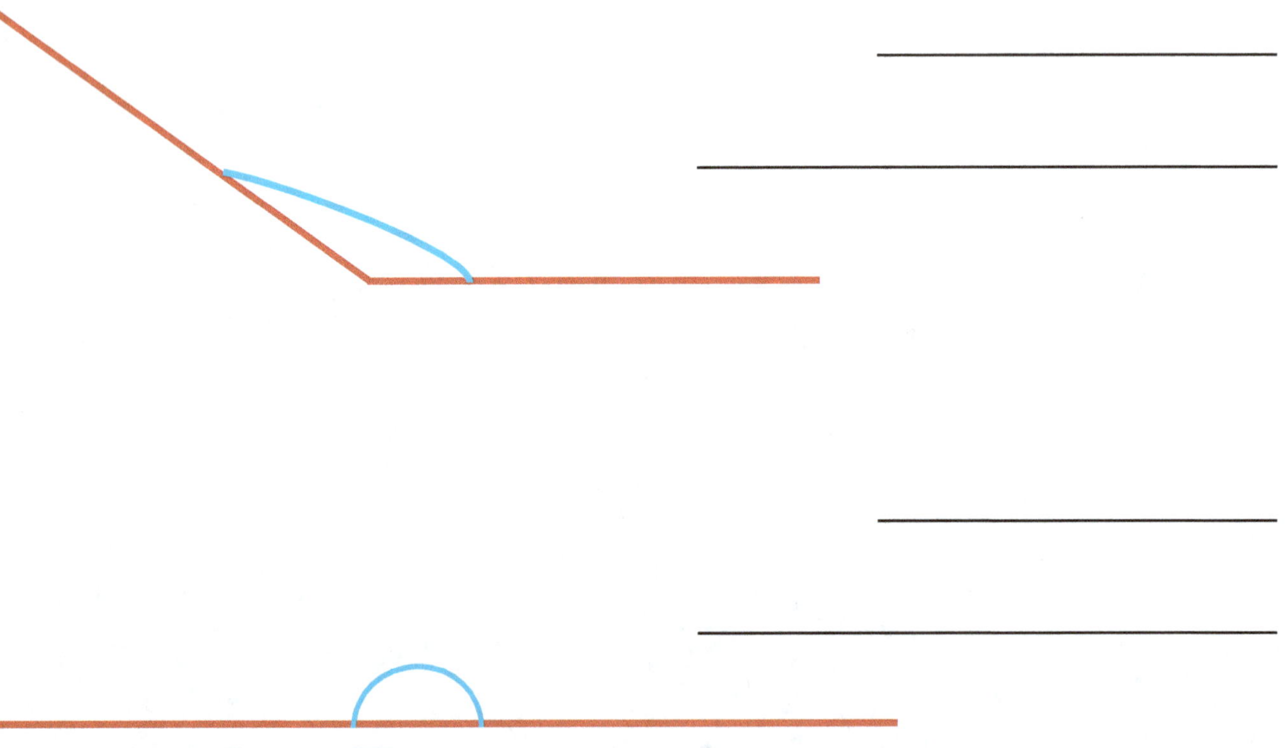

____

____

____

____

GEOMETRY

Measure the angle and name what type of angle.

____

____

GEOMETRY

Draw the angle and name what type of angle.

1. 113° ______________________________

2. 49° ______________________________

GEOMETRY

Draw the angle and name what type of angle.

3. 65°   _______________________

4. 148°   _______________________

Draw the angle and name what type of angle.

5. 223° _______________________________

6. 90° _______________________________

GEOMETRY

Draw the angle and name what type of angle.

7. 180° _________________________________

8. 256° _________________________________

GEOMETRY

Draw the angle and name what type of angle.

9. 45° __________________________

10. 104° __________________________

GEOMETRY

Draw the angle and name what type of angle.

11. 300° ________________________

12. 62° ________________________

GEOMETRY

Draw the angle and name what type of angle.

13. 160° _______________________

14. 34° _______________________

GEOMETRY

Draw the angle and name what type of angle.

15. 128° ___________________________

16. 100° ___________________________

GEOMETRY

Draw the angle and name what type of angle.

17. 95° ______________________

18. 102° ______________________

ANSWERS

1/3 + 1/2 = 5/6

1/6 + 4/5 = 29/30

5/5 + 3/5 = 8/5 or 1 3/5

7/7 + 5/7 = 12/7 or 1 5/7

5/7 + 3/7 = 8/7 or 1 1/7

4/9 + 2/9 = 6/9 or 2/3

2/3 + 2/2= 5/3

3/6 + 1/6 = 4/6 or 2/3

2/6 + 5/5 = 4/3 or 1/3

2/8 + 7/7 = 5/4 or 1 1/4

1/6 + 6/7= 7/7 or 1

7/9 + 4/9 = 11/9 or 1 2/9

1/4 + 2/3 = 11/12

5/6 + 3/6 = 8/6 or 1 1/3

4/6 + 2/6 = 6/6 or 1

5/8 + 3/8 = 8/8 or 1

4/8 + 2/8 =6/8 or 3/4

8/9 + 6/9= 14/9 or 1 2/3

2/3 + 1/5 = 13/15

1/3 + 2/3 = 3/3 or 1

4/5 + 2/7 = 38/35 or 1 3/35

1/4 + 2/5 = 13/20

3/5 + 1/3 = 14/15

1/5 + 1/6 = 11/30

1/3 + 2/3 = 3/3 or 1

3/4 + 4/5 = 31/20 or 1 11/20

2/5 + 1/5 = 3/5

4/7 + 4/6 = 26/21 or 1 5/21

1/8 + 2/3 = 19/24

3/9 + 2/5 = 11/15

3/4 + 4/9 = 43/36 or 1 7/36

4/7 + 6/7 = 10/7 or 1 4/7

8/9 + 3/4 = 59/36 or 1 23/36

3/4 + 3/4 = 6/4 or 1 1/2

1/4 + 3/4 = 4/4 or 1

4/6 + 6/7 = 32/21 or 1 11/21

Acute Angle

Right Angle

Obtuse Angle

Straight Angle

Reflex Angle

1. obtuse angle

2. acute angle

3. acute angle

4. obtuse angle

5. reflex angle

6. right angle

7. straight angle

8. reflex angle

9. acute angle

10. obtuse angle

11. reflex angle

12. acute angle

13. obtuse angle

14. acute angle

15. obtuse angle

16. obtuse angle

17. obtuse angle

18. obtuse angle

9 798886 945183